I Lived in Texas Before it Was Texas

A Child's Life at Mission Espada, San Antonio, Texas 1762

By Robyn Asherman and Marina Rizo-Patron

Illustrator ~ Robyn Asherman

Missions and Forts Press, Inc. Wapiti, Wyoming

First Printing
Missions and Forts Press, Inc.
Wapiti, Wyoming
Copyright © 2004 Missions and Forts Press, Inc.
Copyright © 1995 Orginal Mission Mural, Robyn Rogers Asherman
Design by Vision West, Powell, Wyoming
Research by Robyn Asherman and Marina Rizo-Patron
Edited by Robyn Asherman, Marina Rizo-Patron and Sabrina Crewe
Printed in the United States of America

All Rights Reserved. Request for permission to reproduce material for other than one time educational purposes should be sent to Missions and Forts Press, Inc.

ISBN 0-9700418-0-2

Library of Congress Control Number: 2003113381

Missions and Forts Press, Inc.
P.O. Box 222
Wapiti, Wyoming 82450

This is my home. I live at Mission Espada.

Within our walls we are safe to live,

work and play.

When my mother was a young girl just like me, she lived with her family in this very same spot beside the San Antonio River.

She remembers when there was no mission here and no walls for protection, a time when her father hunted for all of their meat.

My mother has many happy memories. On cool autumn mornings she would share mulberries with the deer, and be very still to go unnoticed by the bears.

Once she climbed the mesquite tree

to escape the wild javelinas.

Now, we live with many families.
My mother tells me stories of her childhood while we work.

We cook.

We spin and weave.

We wash at the river.

**In the spring we gather the green nopalitos from the prickly pear cactus.
My mother tells me to eat all my nopalito for it will make me strong.**

**Bees make delicious honey from the prickly pear flowers.
Once, my father chopped down a hollow oak tree and found where the bees hid their honey.**

**I like to gather the cochineal bugs from the prickly pear in the summer.
I squish the sticky, tiny white bugs between my fingers to see the bright red color.**

My mother uses the cochineal to dye our wool and she always saves a few bugs for me. I like to paint pictures on my skin with the red color.

The men of our mission have much work to do. They shoe our horses and forge our tools.

My brothers tend the sheep and shear their wool for us to spin and weave.

My father works in the garden to grow our vegetables.

**The missionary father is my friend.
He says we must be thankful for all that we have and work together and share.**

So, I take water to the thirsty men. The strong walls that they build protect us.

This is my home.
I live at Mission Espada by
the San Antonio River.

Este es mi hogar.
Vivo en la misión Espada
cerca del río San Antonio.

English Vocabulary
Vocabulario en Español

ax	hacha
ball	pelota
basket	canasta
bees	abejas
bell	campana
bellows	fuelle
blacksmith	herrero
bow & arrow	arco y flecha
bowl	tazón
boy	niño
bugs	bichos
bush	arbusto
butterfly	mariposa
cactus	cactus
carpenter	carpintero
cart	carreta
clothes	ropa
corn	maíz
cotton	algodon
donkey	burro
door	puerta
family	familia
fire	fuego
flower	flor
food	comida
friend	amigo
girl	niña
gourd	chacual
griddle	comal
hammer	martillo
hatchet	hacha
hawk	halcón
hoe	azadón
honey	miel
horseshoe	herradura
leaf	hoja
loom	telar
man	hombre
oven	horno
peach	durazno
plant	planta
pond	estanque
pot	olla
potato	papa
river	río
rooster	gallo
saw	serrucho
shepherd	pastor
skirt	falda
sky	cielo
smoke	humo
stone	piedra
sword	espada
Texas	Tejas
tree	árbol
wall	muro
watermelon	sandia
weaver	tejedora
window	ventana
wool	lana
work	trabajo
yoke	yugo

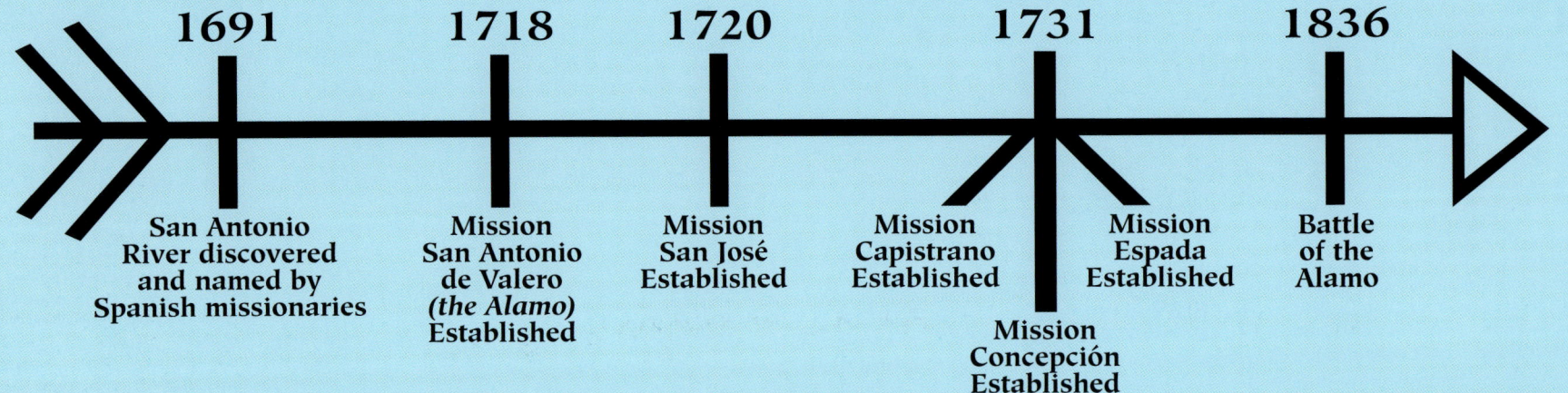

1691	1718	1720	1731	1836
San Antonio River discovered and named by Spanish missionaries	Mission San Antonio de Valero *(the Alamo)* Established	Mission San José Established	Mission Capistrano Established / Mission Espada Established / Mission Concepción Established	Battle of the Alamo

Things To Do

The Missions of San Antonio
San Antonio de Valero 1718
San José 1720
Capistrano 1731
Concepción 1731
Espada 1731

Mission San Francisco de la Espada
Inspiration for "A Child's Life at Mission Espada". Espada is the furthest mission down river from the city of San Antonio. It is famous for its irrigation system.

The Alamo
Site of the world famous 1836 Battle for Texas Independence. The Alamo was founded as the Spanish mission San Antonio de Valero in 1718.

The Witte Museum
Visitors will experience the History, Science and Culture of Texas and its people and children can explore a huge interactive Science Tree House.

Five Spanish missions were built along the banks of the San Antonio River. The mission Indians built irrigation canals that brought water from the river to the mission farm lands.

For thirteen days during the Battle of the Alamo, the men, women and children trapped behind the walls of the Alamo had fresh water because of the old irrigation canal built by the original Mission de Valero Indians in 1718.

Mission Espada has the oldest water irrigation system in the United States still in use today.

In San Antonio

The San Antonio Museum of Art
A restored 19 century brewery exhibiting elaborate collections of Egyptian and Roman Art and the first class Nelson A. Rockefeller Center for Latin American Art.

The San Antonio Children's Museum
The location of the mural Mission Espada presented in "A Child's Life At Mission Espada". The Museum offers a unique and fun learning experience for children and their grownups.

The Buckhorn Saloon and Museum
Spectacular western and wildlife museum in the heart of downtown San Antonio.

The San Antonio Zoo
Surrounded by natural settings, the San Antonio Zoo presents one of the largest collections of animals in America.

The San Antonio Botanical Center
Beautiful conservatories, wandering gardens and a secret lake habitat for native plants and creatures.

Terms and Definitions

San Francisco de la Espada is the name of the fifth mission to be built in the 1700s by the Spanish missionaries and the mission Indians along the San Antonio River. Espada had a ranch where all of its cattle and sheep and horses were kept. It also had a large farm where the mission Indians grew corn, beans, squash, potatoes, melons and many other fruits and vegetables for the mission compound.

Mission is the name for an outpost or a village far away from any other village. Espada was built by Spanish Franciscans so that Native American peoples would become Spanish citizens. The Native Americans, or Indians, would be taught the Catholic religion, the Spanish language and how to farm and build.

Mission compounds were designed on the same plans as medieval fortresses in Europe. They were strong enclosed "villages" with three foot thick walls eight feet high. These "villages" had rooms for the Indian families who lived there. There was always a church and work rooms and storage rooms for food and supplies.

Missionary fathers were priests from the Catholic order of Franciscan Friars. They were the men who built the Spanish missions in Texas and who taught the Indians the Spanish way of life.

Coahuiltecan Indians were the Native Americans who lived in the area around the San Antonio River. They called the river "Yanaguana" which meant "refreshing waters". These were the people who lived at the missions in San Antonio.

White-tailed deer are small mammals that lived in groups around the mission areas. They are quiet and shy and they like to eat berries, grass and mesquite beans. Sometimes the mission Indians tamed the deer as pets.

Black Bears are medium sized mammals that like to climb trees and eat berries all summer long. Their noses are straight and pointy and they use them to smell out honey combs. There aren't any more black bears at the missions, but they used to roam in the woods by the San Antonio River.

Mesquite Trees were the most important food for all the animals and creatures that lived in the countryside by the missions. The mission Indians used every part of the mesquite tree from its roots to its beans. Shake a bunch of dried mesquite bean pods and make great musical sounds!

Javelinas are really scary wild pigs. They have short snouts with huge fangs. Their hair is long and very rough. They travel together in groups and sleep under the prickly pear bushes. They like to eat mesquite beans, sotol cactus and prickly pears.

Nopalitos are very good tasting green pads of the prickly pear cactus. The mission Indians cooked the green pads and served them as a nutritious meal to their families.

Cochineal is the name of the very small bug found on the prickly pear cactus in late summer. The bugs are picked or scraped off and then boiled to get a beautiful scarlet color for dying cloth. The bugs can also be squished to make a tattoo dye. Cochineal is still used today as a food and make-up dye.

The symbol used to brand the horses and cattle belonging to Mission Espada. It was made from iron in the mission blacksmith shop. The vaqueros, or mission cowboys, had to brand the animals.

Facade is the word used to describe the front of a building. The facade of Mission Espada is very famous because the stones of the arch were put in upside-down when it was built.

Tracks
Huellas

 Coahuiltecan Indian / indio coahuilteco

 black bear / oso negro

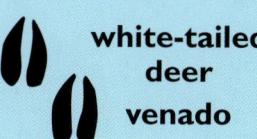 white-tailed deer / venado

 chicken / gallina

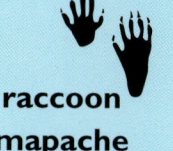 raccoon / mapache

 sheep / oveja

 coyote / coyote

 lizard / lagartija

 pig / puerco

 turtle / tortuga

 buffalo / búfalo

 squirrel / ardilla

 mouse / ratón

 turkey / guajalote

 goose / ganso

 alligator / caimán

 snake / serpiente

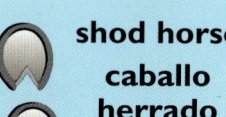 shod horse / caballo herrado

 unshod horse / caballo desherrado

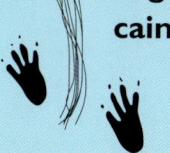 rabbit / conejo

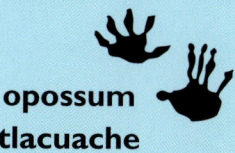 opossum / tlacuache

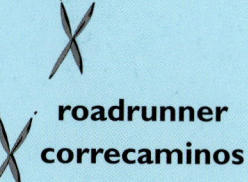 roadrunner / correcaminos

 duck / pato

 ox / buey"

Acknowledgments

Missions and Forts Press, Inc. expresses its appreciation and thanks to those who have inspired and guided the publication of this project.

The San Antonio Children's Museum, San Antonio, Texas for creating a discovery museum about the City of San Antonio and its cultural and natural history.

Vision West, Powell Wyoming, for its leadership and creative staff.

Sherwood Inkley, Photographer, San Antonio, Texas, for his photography of the original Mission Espada mural for this book and the companion CD. We recognize his creativity and his insistence on quality.

Dr. Rosalind Z. Rock, Park Historian of the San Antonio Missions National Historical Park, for her time and expertise on the subject of the San Antonio Missions.

Patty Leslie Pazstor, Botany and Wildlife consultant, San Antonio, Texas, for her generous assistance with the identification and classification of native plants and creatures.

Our families, the Ashermans and the Rizo-Patrons for not saying "No!" to our project.

Bibliography

Davis, William B., & David J. Schmidly. 1994. *The Mammals of Texas*. Austin. Texas Parks and Wildlife.

Wrede, Jan. *Texans Love Their Land. A Guide to 76 Native Texas Hill Country Woody Plants*. 1997. San Antonio. The Watercress Press.

Taylor, Richard B., and Jimmy Rutledge and Joe G. Herrera. *A Field Guide To Common Texas Shrubs*. 1999. Austin. Texas Parks and Wildlife.

Guerra, Mary Ann Noonan. *The Missions of San Antonio*. 1982. San Antonio. The Alamo Press.

Baldridge, Carol. *Texas Missions Fact Cards*. California. Toucan Valley Publication, Inc.

Tull, Delena. *Edible and Useful Plants of Texas and the Southwest: A Practicle Guide*. 1987. Austin. University Of Texas Press.

Jr. League of San Antonio, Inc. *The San Antonio Missions National Historical Park: A Guidebook*. 1986. San Antonio. The Jr. League of San Antonio, Inc.